GIRL
DINNER

GIRL DINNER

85 snack plates & hassle-free meals

ALEJANDRA DIAZ-IMLAH & JAMISON DIAZ-IMLAH

CIDER MILL PRESS

BOOK PUBLISHERS

CONTENTS

WELCOME TO *GIRL DINNER,* WHERE SIMPLICITY AND STYLE COMBINE TO HELP YOU TRANSFORM YOUR EVERYDAY MOMENTS INTO EXTRAORDINARY OCCASIONS.

If you love good food but want to avoid spending hours in the kitchen, or if you enjoy presenting your dishes with a touch of creativity, then you're in the right place.

Our collection of girl dinners will guide you in crafting stunning dishes with minimal effort, and help you master everything from preparation to presentation. We understand that life is full of moments worth celebrating, whether it's a cozy night in, a spontaneous gathering with friends, or a response to the shape a particular day ends up taking.

In this cookbook, you'll find a treasure trove of easy-to-follow recipes that are delicious and visually appealing. But our cookbook goes beyond the basics—it's also a guide to elevating your culinary creations through artful plating and styling techniques. We inspire you to turn simple ingredients into visually stunning masterpieces, ensuring that every dish is not only a delight to eat but also a feast for the eyes.

From stylishly arranged snack plates to creatively presented full meals, each recipe is a testament to the belief that elegance can be achieved without sacrificing accessibility. We've curated this collection keeping different occasions in mind, providing you with versatile recipes that suit various celebrations. Whether you're hosting a casual brunch, a laid-back dinner party, or a festive holiday gathering, our cookbook has got you covered.

So, join us on a journey where minimal effort makes a maximum impact and where the art of presentation beautifully complements the joy of cooking. This is your go-to guide for turning ordinary moments into extraordinary memories—one stylish and delicious plate at a time.

WHAT IS "GIRL DINNER"?

Girl dinner is a simple meal made by arranging ingredients that are readily available in the store or kitchen pantry. It started on TikTok when a user named Olivia Maher responded to a video mocking medieval peasants who had to eat bread and cheese for dinner. Olivia's response was simple—"But that's my dinner!"—and the girl dinner was born.

Over 1.2 million people have now viewed Olivia's video, where she displays a wooden board with two slices of bread, two slices of cheese, four grapes pulled from a nearby bag, butter on a napkin, a glass of wine, and a jar of cornichons, and brands her creation "girl dinner" or "medieval peasant."

After Olivia's video, people started making their versions of girl dinners. Some are mac and cheese served in a wine glass with a Dino Nugget, while others are elaborate plates of fresh veggies paired with charcuterie and cheeses.

As you go through the pages of this cookbook, you'll find that we have created an array of girl dinners that range from no-prep to medium-prep, but always feature easy-to-find ingredients. While the traditional trend of girl dinners tends to focus on meals that are more like snack plates, our recipes take the conventional idea of girl dinner and elevate it, using our culinary expertise to maintain the convenience that is essential to it.

We understand that sometimes we prefer lighter meals, while at other times we may crave something more comforting or protein-heavy. For the most part, you'll find that our recipes follow a traditional meal structure, incorporating starch, protein, fat, and carbs, although this may not be the case for every recipe.

THE ESSENTIALS OF GIRL DINNER

A well-stocked kitchen is the key to successful and enjoyable cooking. Girl dinners often involve combining different ingredients or using those that require minimal preparation or cooking. In this cookbook, we aim to keep things simple while transforming ordinary ingredients into delicious girl-dinner meals.

We suggest keeping some essential ingredients in your pantry so that you can always make a quick and tasty girl dinner at home. Extra-virgin olive oil is a versatile and healthy cooking oil that you should always have, along with herbs and spices like salt, pepper, garlic powder, and dried oregano. Dry goods such as rice, pasta, and different grains provide a solid base for various recipes. Canned goods like tomatoes, beans, and broth add flavor and convenience to your meals. In your refrigerator, make sure you have eggs, butter, and a selection of cheeses on hand. Fresh produce like onions, garlic, and various fruits and vegetables adds vibrant flavors to your dishes and contributes to a balanced and nutritious diet.

THE POWER OF THE FREEZER

Embracing the convenience of frozen food mixes, particularly those crafted with clean and wholesome ingredients, is a game changer for girl dinners. These frozen mixes save valuable prep time and ensure that you're incorporating a rainbow of flavors in your meals. Whether you're whipping up a quick stir-fry, enhancing a soup, or adding a burst of color and nutrients to a pasta dish, frozen food blends are a powerful culinary ally, supplying convenience, nutrition, and flavor.

CHARCUTERIE & CHEESE

Keeping a selection of cured meats, cheeses, and deli meats in your refrigerator is akin to having a culinary tool kit that can effortlessly elevate any meal. These ingredients add depth of flavor to various dishes and provide a quick and convenient source of nutrition. Whether you're creating a charcuterie board, crafting a hearty sandwich, or enhancing the flavor profile of a pasta or salad, these ingredients are wonderful places to turn.

Cured meats contribute a savory and indulgent touch, while cheeses provide a creamy and rich counterpoint. Deli meats, whether sliced thin and rolled up individually or stacked in generous piles, supply a protein boost that can transform everyday dishes into satisfying and nutritionally balanced creations. Having these staples at your fingertips opens a world of possibilities for the girl dinner devotee.

PAIRING INGREDIENTS
AND CAPTURING A THEME

We love curating girl dinners to suit various occasions and themes, as it's a fun and easy way to make your meals more exciting. Our book includes over 80 meals, so we've provided a quick guide below to help you choose the right ingredients for a specific occasion.

FOR A DINNER ENJOYED AL FRESCO:
Consider a mix of flavors for a casual outdoor occasion with a relaxed atmosphere—like guacamole paired with pico de gallo and served with tortilla chips.

FOR A SOPHISTICATED EVENING:
Choose premium options and pair them with complementary flavors: for example, a mushroom cream pappardelle pasta with truffle oil.

FOR A ROMANTIC VIBE:
Pair savory and sweet ingredients and incorporate a number of fruits. An example is bite-sized crostini with creamy Boursin cheese and sweet fruit preserves, topped with prosciutto roses.

FOR A FALL GATHERING:
Embrace the coziness of fall with comforting elements, such as pumpkin ravioli, or a warm squash salad paired with slices from a crisp apple.

FOR A HOLIDAY PARTY:
Celebrate the season with festive ingredients: for example, cranberry cheese on toasted sourdough with pecans, dried fruit, and fresh apples.

STYLING A GIRL DINNER

Styling food is an art that transcends taste, captivating both the eyes and the palate. Elevating the visual appeal of dishes involves the techniques listed below. These tips are good to keep in mind whenever you're putting together a girl dinner, but don't be afraid to go beyond their boundaries and really get creative when putting a meal together!

LEVERAGE COLOR:
Play with color contrasts by incorporating vibrant vegetables or edible flowers, transforming the plate into a canvas full of multicolored hues.

USE TEXTURE AND POSITIONING:
Experiment with various textures, arranging crisp and smooth components beside each other for an engaging sensory experience. Embrace asymmetry to create a visually dynamic presentation that encourages exploration from different angles.

CHOOSE UNIQUE SERVING VESSELS:
Adding personality to each creation can be achieved using unconventional serving vessels such as rustic wooden boards, elegant slate plates, or wineglasses.

PLAY WITH GARNISHES:
Adding sauces, drizzles, and garnishes enhances flavor and elevates an ordinary dish into a culinary masterpiece.

Overall, remember that the essence of food styling lies in embracing imagination and breaking free from convention. Do that, and you'll soon see how to transform each and every meal into an aesthetically pleasing experience.

QUICK COMFORT

NOTHING SAYS "COMFORT FOOD" LIKE MEALS THAT REQUIRE LITTLE TO NO WORK. FROM BREAKFAST FOR DINNER TO CLASSIC CHARCUTERIE TO NOSTALGIC CHILDHOOD DINNERS REVISITED, THIS CHAPTER IS A WEALTH OF DISHES TO SOOTHE THE SOUL. WHETHER YOU'RE AT THE END OF A HARD DAY OR TAKING A MOMENT TO RELAX AND TREAT YOURSELF, COMFORT FOOD IS ALWAYS A SUREFIRE WAY TO RAISE YOUR SPIRITS AND NOURISH YOUR BODY. JUST REST AND ENJOY A SIMPLE AND DELICIOUS MEAL.

A ROSE IS A ROSE IS A ROSE

Some nights, all you want is a few bites of something, but you want each one to be transcendent. The luscious sweetness of the figs, paired with the rich, salty prosciutto more than meets this call.

5 FRESH FIGS

4 SLICES OF PROSCIUTTO

FRESH THYME, FOR GARNISH

FRESH SAGE, FOR GARNISH

BALSAMIC VINEGAR, FOR DRIZZLING

Quarter the figs and place them on your serving dish or board.

Stack 2 slices of prosciutto and twist them into a long strand. Wrap the strand of prosciutto around itself to form a rosette and place it in the center of one of the quartered figs. Repeat with the remaining prosciutto and then set it in the center of another fig.

Garnish with thyme and sage, drizzle some balsamic vinegar over the top, and enjoy.

COMFY COZY

Comforting, sure. But the crispy broccoli and cauliflower cut beautifully against the creaminess of the mac and cheese bites, and provide enough nutrition to clear away any possibility of guilt over selecting an appetizer as dinner.

1 BAG OF FROZEN MAC AND CHEESE BITES

1 BAG OF FROZEN BROCCOLI AND CAULIFLOWER BLEND

EXTRA-VIRGIN OLIVE OIL, AS NEEDED

SALT AND PEPPER, TO TASTE

KETCHUP, FOR SERVING

Cook the mac and cheese bites according to the directions on the package.

Preheat an air fryer to 400°F and coat the basket with nonstick cooking spray.

Place the broccoli and cauliflower in the basket, drizzle olive oil over the top, and season with salt and pepper. Toss to coat and air fry the broccoli until it is crispy but tender, 15 to 25 minutes, stirring halfway through.

Arrange the vegetables and mac and cheese bites on a plate and serve with ketchup.

BREAKFAST FOR DINNER

If you're one of those gals who think breakfast works anytime, this meal's for you.

FROZEN WAFFLES, AS DESIRED

WHIPPED CREAM, FOR TOPPING

STRAWBERRY JAM, FOR TOPPING

FRESH STRAWBERRIES, SLICED, FOR TOPPING

MAPLE SYRUP, FOR DRIZZLING

Toast the waffles and then let them cool for 1 minute.

Cut the waffles lengthwise into rectangles and arrange them on a plate.

Top each waffle with whipped cream, strawberry jam, and strawberries, drizzle maple syrup over the top, and enjoy.

TOTAL TIME: 10 MINUTES

FAR FROM BOARD

The beauty of the charcuterie board is its ability to supply variety and balance effortlessly—in other words, the ideal vehicle for a girl dinner.

¼ CUP MINIATURE MOZZARELLA BALLS

¼ CUP GLAZED NUTS

4 TO 6 SLICES OF CHEDDAR CHEESE

1 TO 3 SLICES OF PROSCIUTTO

3 TO 5 SLICES OF SALAMI

2 PITTED DATES

Arrange all of the ingredients on a board, getting creative with how you curate them. Mixing and matching the cheese and cured meats, and placing the nuts and mozzarella balls in small ramekins is just one idea!

UNDER THE TUSCAN SUN

A good one to turn to on a sweltering summer night when the thought of standing by the stove for any amount of time is horrifying. For the pickled vegetables, giardiniera is a solid option.

6 TO 8 MARINATED OLIVES, PITTED

¼ CUP MINIATURE MOZZARELLA BALLS

4 TO 6 CORNICHONS

PICKLED VEGETABLES, AS DESIRED

4 CHERRY TOMATOES

6 SLICES OF SALAMI

2 SLICES OF PROSCIUTTO

1 TABLESPOON PICKLED RELISH

¼ CUP SHREDDED CHEDDAR CHEESE

Arrange two small ramekins on opposite sides of a plate. Place the olives in one ramekin and the mozzarella balls in the other.

Arrange some of the cornichons and pickled vegetables and all of the cherry tomatoes in between the ramekins.

Fold the salami into quarters and arrange them on one side of the plate.

Twist the prosciutto and arrange them on the opposite side of the plate from the salami.

Arrange the relish, cheddar cheese, and remaining cornichons and pickled vegetables on the outer edge of the plate and enjoy.

HOLEY ART THOU

Perfection should not be so simple as spiking a cream cheese with dill, spreading that atop a toasted bagel, and adding a trio of entirely complementary toppings. Fortunately for you, it is.

2 OZ. CREAM CHEESE, PLUS MORE AS NEEDED

ZEST OF ½ LEMON

1 TEASPOON FINELY CHOPPED FRESH DILL, PLUS MORE FOR GARNISH

SALT AND PEPPER, TO TASTE

1 EVERYTHING BAGEL

2 TO 3 SLICES OF SMOKED SALMON

1 TABLESPOON CAPERS

¼ ONION, SLICED

Place the cream cheese, lemon zest, and dill in the work bowl of a stand mixer fitted with the paddle attachment and beat on high until the cream cheese is fluffy.

Scrape down the work bowl, season the cream cheese with salt and pepper, and beat for 30 seconds to combine.

Slice the bagel in half and toast it. Spread some cream cheese on the bagel. Top one half with the smoked salmon and top the other with the capers and onion.

Garnish with additional dill and enjoy.

NOSTALGIA, REFINED

There are times when the cravings of childhood return with force. When they do, it's best to embrace them, and introduce them to your new, more elegant self.

1 (6 OZ.) BOX OF MAC AND CHEESE

Cook the mac and cheese according to the directions on the package.

Transfer the prepared mac and cheese to an elegant vessel—a coupe or a wineglass—and enjoy.

TONIGHT, WE'RE TIMELESS

Yes, you're a grown woman. But that doesn't mean that the PB & J has become any less perfect.

1½ TEASPOONS UNSALTED BUTTER

2 SLICES OF BRIOCHE

2 TABLESPOONS CREAMY PEANUT BUTTER

1½ TABLESPOONS STRAWBERRY JELLY

½ BANANA, SLICED

Place the butter in a large skillet and melt it over medium heat. Add the bread to the skillet and toast until it is a light golden brown on one side.

Carefully remove the bread from the pan and place it on a cutting board. Let it cool briefly.

Spread the peanut butter over the untoasted side of one piece of bread and the jelly over the untoasted side of the other. Top the peanut butter with the banana and then assemble the sandwich. Cut it in half and enjoy.

TAKEOUT TAKEOVER

With so many food delivery apps available, it's always tempting to opt for takeout when you want something quick and comforting. But resist the urge and whip up this dinner, which is just as tasty and has a far more attractive price tag.

1 SERVING OF FROZEN POTSTICKERS

¼ CUP PONZU SAUCE

½ CUP SHELLED EDAMAME

SALT, TO TASTE

Cook the potstickers according to the directions on the package.

Place the ponzu in a ramekin. Place the edamame in a separate ramekin and season it with salt.

Arrange the potstickers on a board or plate, place the ponzu and edamame beside them, and enjoy.

STAY AWAKE
(LATE NIGHT)

There are nights where you know goings-on are going to extend into the early hours of the morning, and on such occasions you need four things: carbs, protein, vitamins, and caffeine. This dinner checks every box, and lets you get on with making the night memorable.

2 PASTRIES

1 PROTEIN BAR

½ CUP CHOPPED FRUIT

COFFEE OR TEA, FOR SERVING

Arrange your pastry, protein bar, and fruit on a plate and enjoy with a cup of coffee or tea.

SOAR TO THE SHORE

Craving seafood but can't make it out to the ocean? No problem, just pair some good crab cakes from the store with homemade fries and let your tastebuds carry your imagination away.

1 RUSSET POTATO

1 TABLESPOON PLUS 1 TEASPOON EXTRA-VIRGIN OLIVE OIL

1 TEASPOON OLD BAY SEASONING, PLUS MORE TO TASTE

SALT, TO TASTE

½ LB. FROZEN CRAB CAKES, THAWED

TARTAR SAUCE, FOR SERVING

Preheat the oven to 400°F and coat a baking sheet with nonstick cooking spray. Place the potato on a cutting board and slice it in half lengthwise. Cut each piece in half lengthwise and then cut each quarter in half so that you have eight steak fries.

Place the fries in a bowl, add the teaspoon of olive oil and Old Bay seasoning, and season them with salt. Toss to combine, place the fries on the baking sheet, and place them in the oven. Bake until they are crispy, golden brown, and cooked through, about 30 minutes.

While the fries are in the oven, warm a large cast-iron skillet over medium heat. Add the remaining olive oil, warm it, and then add the crab cakes, taking care to avoid the oil if it spatters. Gently press down on the crab cakes to flatten them slightly.

Reduce the heat to medium-low and cook until the bottoms of the crab cakes are golden brown, 4 to 5 minutes. Flip the crab cakes over and cook until they are golden brown and cooked through (the internal temperature is 135°F), 3 to 4 minutes.

Remove the fries from the oven, season them with salt and Old Bay seasoning, and arrange them on a plate with the crab cakes. Serve with tartar sauce and enjoy.

THE HAPPIEST HOUR

When happy hour hits but the quiet of your home seems so much more appealing than a noisy bar, turn to this collection of snacks and your favorite cocktail.

¼ CUP HUMMUS

4 PITA CHIPS

¼ CUP NUTS

PREFERRED COCKTAIL, FOR SERVING

Place the hummus in a small bowl or ramekin and top with the pita chips.

Serve with nuts and your favorite cocktail and enjoy.

THIS IS PARADISE

Not every meal can be spent dining out at fancy restaurants, but that doesn't mean you have to forgo great taste and elegant plating. Enjoy a dish that looks and tastes just as good as the plates at your favorite splurge spot, without the painful price point!

¼ CUP SHREDDED NAPA CABBAGE

SALT, TO TASTE

4 TO 6 OZ. LEFTOVER ROASTED PORK BELLY

2 TABLESPOONS THINLY SLICED RED ONION

¼ CUP DICED PINEAPPLE, RESERVE ANY JUICES

2 TABLESPOONS CHOPPED FRESH CILANTRO

Preheat the oven to 400°F and coat a baking sheet with nonstick cooking spray.

Place the cabbage on the pan, season it with salt, and arrange the pork belly on top of the cabbage.

Place the baking sheet in the oven and roast until the cabbage has browned and the pork belly is crispy and warmed through, 25 to 30 minutes.

Remove the pan from the oven and arrange the cabbage on a plate. Top it with the red onion, pineapple, and cilantro, set the pork belly on top, and enjoy.

LATIN-INSPIRED LUXURY

The pupusa and arepa are two of Latin America's greatest culinary exports. When brightened by the slaw and salsa, they make for a memorable dinner.

1 FROZEN PUPUSA

1 FROZEN CORN & CHEESE AREPA

¼ CUP PICKLED VEGGIE SLAW

1 TABLESPOON SALSA ROJA

ARUGULA, FOR SERVING (OPTIONAL)

Cook the pupusa and arepa according to the directions on their packages.

Arrange the pupusa and arepa on a board, serve alongside the slaw, salsa, and arugula (if desired), and enjoy.

BROKE MADAME

Using the beloved "Egg in the Hole" technique to combine the egg and bread supplies a fun, elevated spin on the classic croque madame.

1 TEASPOON UNSALTED BUTTER, PLUS MORE AS NEEDED

2 SLICES OF SOURDOUGH BREAD

1 TEASPOON DIJON MUSTARD

1 TABLESPOON SHREDDED CHEDDAR CHEESE

3 TO 4 SLICES OF TURKEY OR HAM

1 EGG

SALT AND PEPPER, TO TASTE

FRUIT, FOR SERVING

Preheat the oven to 400°F and coat a small baking sheet with butter.

Place one of the slices of sourdough bread on the pan and spread the mustard over it. Sprinkle cheese on top of the bread, top it with the turkey or ham, and place it in the oven. Bake until the bottom of the bread is toasted and the cheese has melted, about 6 minutes.

While the bread is toasting, place the butter in a skillet and melt it over medium heat. Use a ring mold to remove the center of the remaining piece of bread. Place the slice of bread in the pan and cook it for 1 minute.

Crack the egg into the hole in the center of the bread and season it with salt and pepper. Cook until the egg white has set, 2 to 3 minutes.

Gently flip the bread and egg over and cook it for another minute. Turn off the heat and leave it in the pan for 30 seconds.

Remove the bread from the oven, top it with the bread with the egg, and enjoy with some fruit on the side.

BOUGIE AF

Cuisine has come a long way since the days when cream of mushroom soup was a kitchen staple. But that doesn't eliminate its effectiveness, as you'll see with this luscious and easy-to-prepare sauce.

SALT AND PEPPER, TO TASTE

2 OZ. PAPPARDELLE

½ (10.5 OZ.) CAN OF CREAM OF MUSHROOM SOUP

½ TEASPOON CANNED TRUFFLES

1 TABLESPOON GRATED PARMESAN CHEESE

Bring a large saucepan of water to a boil. Add salt and the pasta and cook until it is al dente, 8 to 10 minutes.

Reserve 2 tablespoons of the pasta water and then drain the pasta.

Add the soup to the pan, add the pasta water, and bring to a simmer.

Add the pasta and truffles to the soup, reduce the heat to low, and cook for 1 to 2 minutes, tossing to combine.

Season with salt and pepper, stir in the Parmesan, and enjoy.

ONE NIGHT IN OAXACA

The gooey character of a quesadilla cries out for something fresh and crunchy, and this colorful salad fits the bill, beautifully rounding out the dish.

1 TABLESPOON EXTRA-VIRGIN OLIVE OIL

3 TO 4 BABY BELL PEPPERS, STEMMED, SEEDED, AND QUARTERED

¼ CUP CORN KERNELS

1 TEASPOON UNSALTED BUTTER

2 CORN TORTILLAS

¼ CUP SHREDDED OAXACAN CHEESE

2 RADISHES, SLICED

3 TO 5 SUN-DRIED TOMATOES IN OLIVE OIL, DRAINED

1 CUP ARUGULA

1 TABLESPOON CILANTRO-LIME DRESSING

Preheat the oven to 400°F and coat a baking sheet with the olive oil. Add the peppers and roast for 15 minutes.

Add the corn to the pan and roast until the corn has browned and the peppers are tender, about 15 minutes.

While the vegetables are roasting, place the butter in a large skillet and melt it over medium heat. Place the tortillas in the pan, top each one with cheese, and cook until the cheese begins to melt, about 3 minutes.

Assemble the quesadillas, putting the cheesy sides of the tortillas together. Cook the quesadilla for 1 minute on each side so that it is golden brown.

Transfer the quesadilla to a cutting board and cut it into wedges.

Remove the peppers and corn from the oven, place the mixture in a bowl, and add the remaining ingredients. Toss to combine, serve the salad alongside the quesadilla, and enjoy.

CHICAGO FIRE

Many think of the Midwest as "Flyover Country," but anyone who has experienced the kindness and creativity of its residents, and the foods that those who emigrated to the region have made staples of the local cuisine, knows that it is well worth celebrating.

1 TABLESPOON EXTRA-VIRGIN OLIVE OIL

¼ CUP THINLY SLICED YELLOW ONION

6 FROZEN PIEROGIES

¼ CUP SAUERKRAUT

2 TABLESPOONS SOUR CREAM

Warm a large skillet over high heat for 1 minute. Add the olive oil and onion and reduce the heat to medium-low. Cook the onion, stirring occasionally, until it starts to brown, about 5 minutes.

Add ⅓ cup water to the pan and gently scrape up any browned bits from the bottom of the pan. Cook until the liquid has evaporated and the onion is a dark golden brown.

Remove the caramelized onion from the pan and set it aside.

Cook the pierogies according to the directions on the package.

Serve the pierogies alongside the caramelized onion, sauerkraut, and sour cream and enjoy.

ALL THE THINGS

Sweet. Savory. Creamy. Crunchy. Plenty of protein. Just the right amount of carbs. This dinner has everything a girl could ever want.

1 SLICE OF SOURDOUGH BREAD

¼ CUP COTTAGE CHEESE

6 TO 8 SLICES OF APPLE

1½ TEASPOONS HONEY

1 TABLESPOON WALNUT HALVES

FLAKY SEA SALT, FOR GARNISH

Toast the bread and place it on a plate.

Spread the cottage cheese over the bread and top it with the apple.

Drizzle the honey over the toast, sprinkle the walnut halves and salt over the top, and enjoy.

PEP RALLY

Combining the gentle sweetness of bell peppers with the all-around greatness of cream cheese is more than enough to compose memorable bites. Topping that dynamic duo is a medley of other accessible ingredients that take this simple dish to the next level.

1 TABLESPOON EXTRA-VIRGIN OLIVE OIL

2 LINKS OF CHICKEN BREAKFAST SAUSAGE

2 BABY BELL PEPPERS, STEMMED, SEEDED, AND HALVED

¼ CUP CREAM CHEESE

1 TABLESPOON FINELY DICED CUCUMBER

½ TEASPOON BLACK PEPPER

½ TEASPOON EVERYTHING SEASONING

½ TEASPOON RED PEPPER FLAKES

½ TEASPOON HONEY

1 MANDARIN, PEELED AND SEGMENTED

NUTS, AS DESIRED

Place the olive oil in a large skillet and warm it over medium heat. Add the sausage and cook until it is cooked through and golden brown all over, 8 to 10 minutes, turning it as necessary. Set the sausage aside.

Fill the bell peppers with the cream cheese. Top one bell pepper with the cucumber and black pepper, one with the everything seasoning, one with the red pepper flakes, and the last bell pepper with the honey.

Arrange the bell peppers, sausage, mandarin, and nuts on a plate and enjoy.

FEEL-GOOD FEAST

When winter descends, nothing warms quite like the pairing of grilled cheese and tomato soup.

1 CUP TOMATO SOUP

2 SLICES OF BREAD

2 SLICES OF CHEESE

2 TABLESPOONS UNSALTED BUTTER

Place the soup in a small saucepan and warm it.

Assemble the sandwich with the bread and cheese. Place a large nonstick skillet on the stove and warm it over medium heat for about 20 seconds. Add 1 tablespoon of butter and melt it.

Place the sandwich in the pan and reduce the heat to medium-low. Cook until the bottom piece of bread is golden brown, 2 to 3 minutes.

Turn the sandwich over, add the remaining butter to the pan, and cook until the sandwich is golden brown on both sides and the cheese has melted.

Serve the soup alongside the grilled cheese and enjoy.

CROU-TON OF FUN

To be fair, no one ever put a limit on how large a crouton can be before it becomes something else. Take advantage of this loophole when the temperatures start to drop and you want something that nourishes and comforts.

1 (10.5 OZ.) CAN OF SOUP

1 SLICE OF SOURDOUGH BREAD

¼ CUP SHAVED PARMESAN CHEESE

FRESH HERBS, AS DESIRED

1 TEASPOON BALSAMIC VINEGAR

Place the soup in a small saucepan and warm it.

Toast the bread and set it aside.

Place the soup in a bowl and top it with the toast. Top the toast with the Parmesan, herbs, and balsamic and enjoy.

NO CLUCKS GIVEN

Is it breakfast? Is it dinner? Is it good? Push all questions to the side and just give yourself over to the genius who decided to pair chicken and waffles together.

2 CHICKEN TENDERLOINS

1 TEASPOON KOSHER SALT

1 TEASPOON BLACK PEPPER

1 TEASPOON FAJITA SEASONING

1 TABLESPOON EXTRA-VIRGIN OLIVE OIL

2 FROZEN WAFFLES

½ CUP ARUGULA

2 TO 3 SUN-DRIED TOMATOES IN OLIVE OIL

MAPLE SYRUP, FOR TOPPING

Season the chicken with the salt, pepper, and fajita seasoning.

Place the olive oil in a large skillet and warm it over medium-high heat. Add the chicken and cook until it is golden brown on both sides and cooked through (the internal temperature is 165°F), 6 to 8 minutes, turning it as necessary.

While the chicken is cooking, toast the waffles.

Remove the chicken from the pan and let it rest for 2 minutes.

Arrange the chicken, waffles, arugula, and sun-dried tomatoes on a plate, drizzle maple syrup over the chicken and waffles, and enjoy.

A WORLD OF PURE IMAGINATION

Real talk: sometimes, the world pushes you to a place where something sweet is all that will do. This dinner is perfect for such moments.

1 PLANTAIN, PEELED AND SLICED

1 TABLESPOON SUGAR

PINCH OF CINNAMON

PINCH OF KOSHER SALT

2 SCOOPS OF DULCE DE LECHE ICE CREAM

WALNUT HALVES, FOR GARNISH

CARAMEL SAUCE, FOR TOPPING

Warm a large skillet over medium-high heat. Place the plantain in a bowl, add the sugar, cinnamon, and salt, and toss to combine.

Add the plantain to the pan and cook until it is browned and caramelized, 4 to 6 minutes, turning it as necessary.

Transfer the plantain to a bowl and top it with the ice cream and walnuts. Drizzle the caramel over the top and enjoy.

EFFORTLESS EXCELLENCE

In a book focused on meals that require very little time spent chopping and standing at the stove supervising, this one just may require the least effort.

1 SERVING OF FROZEN VEGGIE CAKES OR ARTICHOKE TIMBALES

2 TO 3 TORTILLA PINWHEELS

Cook the cakes or timbales according to the directions on the package.

Arrange the tortilla pinwheels on a plate and serve them alongside the cakes or timbales.

ALL WORK AND NO PLAY

There will be times our jobs overstep their boundaries and begin making unreasonable demands. In such moments, it's important to not just reach for whatever's quick, but take a moment, step away from the computer entirely, and make yourself something a little more special, something that rewards your extra effort with each bite, such as this toast.

1 SLICE OF SOURDOUGH BREAD

1 BURRATA

FLESH OF ¼ AVOCADO, SLICED

2 TO 3 SUN-DRIED TOMATOES IN OLIVE OIL

1 CUP ARUGULA

1 TABLESPOON EXTRA-VIRGIN OLIVE OIL

8 TO 10 SLICES OF SALAMI

¼ CUP NUTS

BLACK PEPPER, TO TASTE

Toast the bread in a toaster or an oven.

Place the toast on a plate and top it with the burrata, avocado, and sun-dried tomatoes.

Place the arugula and olive oil in a bowl and toss to combine. Transfer the salad to the plate and add the salami and nuts.

Crack some black pepper over the toast and enjoy.

LET HER COOK

This dinner takes longer to prepare than any other in the book, but don't go looking elsewhere just yet—most of that time is hands-off, and in the end you'll have a meal that provides far more than just fuel.

FOR THE CHOPPED SALAD

½ CUP CHOPPED BIBB LETTUCE

1 TEASPOON CHOPPED CUCUMBER

1 TEASPOON CHOPPED COOKED BACON

1 TEASPOON CHOPPED TOMATOES

1 TEASPOON CRUMBLED BLUE CHEESE

PREFERRED DRESSING, AS DESIRED

SALT AND PEPPER, TO TASTE

FOR THE LOADED POTATO

1 RUSSET POTATO

SALT, TO TASTE

1½ TABLESPOONS SOUR CREAM

1 TEASPOON DICED COOKED BACON

1 TEASPOON FINELY CHOPPED
FRESH CHIVES

1 TEASPOON SHREDDED
CHEDDAR CHEESE

6 TO 8 OZ. STEAK

SALT AND PEPPER, TO TASTE

Place all of the ingredients for the salad in a bowl and toss to combine. Transfer the salad to the plate and chill it in the refrigerator.

Preheat the oven to 375°F. Place the potato in the oven and bake it until a knife inserted into passes easily to the center, about 1 hour.

When the potato is nearly done, season the steak with salt and pepper and cook it until it is the desired level of doneness (the internal temperature should be 125°F for medium-rare).

Remove the potato from the oven and slice it lengthwise in the center, making sure not to cut through either end.

Gently push the ends together to open the potato, season it with salt, and add the sour cream, bacon, chives, and cheese. Place the steak and potato on the plate beside the salad and enjoy.

A SUMMER'S DAY

Shall I compare thee to a summer's day? Well, it would be a pretty odd comparison, but this burger certainly brings all the joy of a relaxing day with perfect weather. Backyard picnic, anyone?

5 OZ. GROUND BEEF BURGER

SALT AND PEPPER, TO TASTE

1 SLICE OF CHEDDAR CHEESE

1 SESAME SEED BUN, SPLIT OPEN

FLESH OF ½ AVOCADO, SLICED

4 TO 5 SLICES OF PICKLED RED ONION

1 LARGE BIBB LETTUCE LEAF

Season the burger with salt and pepper and cook it on the stove or grill until it is just about cooked through.

Top the patty with the cheese and cook until the burger is completely cooked through and the cheese has melted. Remove the burger from the pan and let it rest.

Lightly toast your bun. Place the avocado on the bottom bun and top it with the burger. Top the burger with the pickled onion and lettuce, assemble the burger with the top bun, and enjoy.

SOMETIMES YOU GET *THE BEAR*

FX's *The Bear* has taken the television world by storm, and this elegant, playful omelet, which Sydney prepared for Natalie in one episode, is just one of many memorable moments from the show's impeccable first two seasons.

3 LARGE EGGS

SALT AND PEPPER, TO TASTE

½ TEASPOON UNSALTED BUTTER

1 TABLESPOON CRUMBLED BOURSIN CHEESE, PLUS MORE TO TASTE

1 TABLESPOON CHOPPED FRESH CHIVES, PLUS MORE TO TASTE

6 LARGE SOUR CREAM & ONION CHIPS, CRUMBLED

Place the eggs in a bowl, season with salt and pepper, and whisk to combine.

Warm a nonstick skillet over over high heat. Add the butter and swirl to coat the pan as it melts. Add the eggs and cook until they start to firm up.

Use a rubber spatula to pull the outer edges toward the center and swirl the pan so that the uncooked eggs move to the edge of the pan. Continue to swirl the pan until the eggs are about three-quarters of the way cooked.

Turn the heat off under the pan and add the Boursin and chives. Fold the omelet over and let it sit in the pan until it has finished cooking and set, 30 to 45 seconds.

Gently transfer the omelet onto a plate. Top it with the chips and additional chives and Boursin and enjoy.

SURPRISE ZINGER

A dinner that will clue you in to your new favorite secret weapon in the kitchen: the sweet tang of peppadew peppers.

¼ CUP PICKLED CABBAGE

2 TABLESPOONS CHOPPED PEPPADEW PEPPERS

1 TABLESPOON MAYONNAISE

1 TEASPOON KETCHUP

¼ TEASPOON DIJON MUSTARD

6 SLICES OF PASTRAMI

Place the cabbage and peppers in a bowl, add the ketchup, mayonnaise, and mustard, and stir to combine.

Divide the pastrami into three stacks of 2 slices.

Divide the sauce between the stacks of pastrami, spreading it over the top slice. Roll up the pastrami, arrange the rolls on a plate, and enjoy.

STUDY ABROAD

Make this Oktoberfest-inspired meal when you need a reminder of those times when you were traveling and discovered all of the wonder the world contained.

1 BRATWURST

¼ CUP SAUERKRAUT

¼ CUP PRETZELS

2 TABLESPOONS MUSTARD

Cook the bratwurst on the stove or in the oven until it is browned all over and cooked through (the internal temperature is 165°F).

Arrange the bratwurst on a plate or a board with the sauerkraut, pretzels, and mustard and enjoy.

GLOW-UP

A GLOW-UP IS A TRANSFORMATION WHERE YOU BECOME A HAPPIER AND MORE CONFIDENT VERSION OF YOURSELF. THAT CAN BE THE RESULT OF SOMETHING AS SMALL AS LISTENING TO YOUR BODY AND GIVING IT THE NOURISHMENT IT NEEDS. SOMETIMES ALL YOU WANT IS TO KEEP IT LIGHT, WITH INGREDIENTS THAT REJUVENATE THE MIND AND BODY. THERE ARE LOTS OF DISHES HERE THAT WILL SATISFY THOSE LOOKING FOR SOMETHING EASY TO ENJOY AFTER A WORKOUT, ON A HOT DAY, OR WHEN YOU'RE JUST CRAVING SOMETHING SIMPLE AND FRESH. AND WHILE THERE IS PLENTY OF GREENERY TO BE FOUND IN THIS CHAPTER, THERE ARE ALSO TONS OF OPPORTUNITIES TO CREATE HEARTY MEALS THAT ARE PACKED WITH PROTEIN. WELLNESS COMES IN ALL SHAPES AND SIZES, AND LEARNING TO FUEL YOUR BODY IN A WAY THAT MAKES YOU FEEL GOOD IS THE GREATEST GLOW-UP OF ALL!

ROLL CALL

Spring rolls are a treat in themselves, but a light and invigorating salad that combines the nutty richness of edamame, the sweetness of carrots, and the tender crispness of broccoli sprouts makes eating healthy easier than ever.

1 BOX OF FROZEN VEGETABLE SPRING ROLLS

1½ TABLESPOONS SESAME OIL

½ CUP SHELLED EDAMAME

1 MEDIUM CARROT, PEELED AND CHOPPED

½ CUP BROCCOLI SPROUTS

½ TEASPOON SOY SAUCE

SALT AND PEPPER, TO TASTE

PREFERRED DIPPING SAUCE, FOR SERVING

Cook the spring rolls according to the directions on the package.

Place 1 tablespoon of sesame oil in a skillet and warm it over medium heat. Add the edamame and cook, stirring occasionally, until it starts to brown, about 3 minutes.

Transfer the edamame to a mixing bowl, add the carrot, broccoli sprouts, soy sauce, and remaining sesame oil, season the mixture with salt and pepper, and toss to combine.

Arrange the spring rolls and salad on a plate and enjoy with your preferred dipping sauce.

NACHO DINNER, MY DINNER

A meal that features all of the treasured flavors present in a plate of nachos, and far more nutrients thanks to a swap of sweet potatoes for the tortilla chips.

1 SWEET POTATO, PEELED AND SLICED

2 TABLESPOONS EXTRA-VIRGIN OLIVE OIL

SALT AND PEPPER, TO TASTE

½ CUP FROZEN CORN

½ (14 OZ.) CAN OF BLACK BEANS, DRAINED

FLESH OF 1 AVOCADO, DICED

¼ CUP PICO DE GALLO

2 TABLESPOONS CRUMBLED COTIJA CHEESE

4 SLICES OF JALAPEÑO CHILE PEPPER, FOR GARNISH

FRESH CILANTRO, FOR GARNISH

Preheat the oven to 425°F and coat a baking sheet with nonstick cooking spray.

Place the sweet potato in a mixing bowl, drizzle half of the olive oil over it, and season it with salt. Toss to coat, arrange the sweet potato on the baking sheet, and place it in the oven.

Bake the sweet potato for 10 minutes, remove the baking sheet from the oven, and turn the sweet potato over.

Bake until the sweet potato is tender and caramelized, 10 to 15 minutes.

While the sweet potato is in the oven, coat a large skillet with the remaining olive oil and warm it over medium heat. Add the corn and cook, stirring occasionally, until it has thawed, about 4 minutes. Season the corn with salt and transfer it to a bowl.

Add the black beans, avocado, and pico de gallo to the corn, season the mixture with salt and pepper, and stir to combine.

Remove the sweet potato from the oven and arrange it on a plate. Top each slice with some of the corn salsa and cotija cheese, garnish with the jalapeño and cilantro, and enjoy.

INDULGENT, INTELLIGENT

Prioritizing health and wellness doesn't mean that you always have to sacrifice flavor, as this spread shows.

1 (12 OZ.) BAG OF FROZEN GARLIC AND PARMESAN ZUCCHINI FRIES

4 CHICKEN TENDERLOINS

SALT AND PEPPER, TO TASTE

1 TABLESPOON ITALIAN SEASONING

1 TABLESPOON GARLIC POWDER

1 TABLESPOON EXTRA-VIRGIN OLIVE OIL

PREFERRED DIPPING SAUCE, FOR SERVING

Bake the zucchini fries according to the directions on the package.

Season the chicken with salt, pepper, and the Italian seasoning and garlic powder.

Place the olive oil in a large skillet and warm it over medium-high heat. Add the chicken, cook until it is golden brown on one side, and turn it over. Cook the chicken until it is cooked through (the internal temperature is 165°F). Remove the chicken from the pan and let it rest for 5 minutes.

Remove the zucchini fries from the oven. Arrange the chicken and zucchini fries on a plate and enjoy with your preferred dipping sauce.

CALIFORNIA LOVE

By pairing creamy avocado with the toothsome texture of tuna and setting it atop a crunchy base comprised of crispbreads and Bibb lettuce, you get a combination that feels like West Coast sunshine on a plate.

1 (5 OZ.) CAN OF TUNA, DRAINED

FLESH OF 1 AVOCADO

JUICE OF ½ LEMON

1 TABLESPOON EXTRA-VIRGIN OLIVE OIL

SALT AND PEPPER, TO TASTE

2 CRISPBREADS

2 LARGE LEAVES OF BIBB LETTUCE

Place the tuna in a bowl and flake it with a fork. Add the avocado, lemon juice, and olive oil and work the mixture with a fork, making sure to lightly mash the avocado.

Season the tuna salad with salt and pepper and stir to incorporate.

Arrange the crispbreads on a plate and top each one with a piece of lettuce. Top the lettuce with the tuna salad and enjoy.

BONANZA

A protein-packed rice bowl that is bursting with flavor thanks to the bright taste of the pineapple and pickled onion and the creamy, subtle sweetness of plantains.

½ CUP MICROWAVABLE WHITE RICE

1 TEASPOON CANOLA OIL

1 RIPE PLANTAIN, PEELED AND SLICED

½ CUP CANNED BLACK BEANS, DRAINED

¼ CUP PINEAPPLE CHUNKS

2 TABLESPOONS CHOPPED PICKLED RED ONION

SALT AND PEPPER, TO TASTE

Cook the rice according to the directions on the package.

Place the canola oil in a large nonstick skillet and warm it over medium heat. Add the plantain and fry for 1½ minutes without turning it over. Turn the plantain over and fry for another minute.

Place the plantain in a bowl, add the rice, beans, pineapple, and pickled onion and season the mixture with salt and pepper. Fold to combine and enjoy.

DIP CAN BE DINNER

Forget the haters. Making a great girl dinner is about taking matters into your own hands and fully embracing those elements that you love. If creamy hummus, tzatziki, and artichoke dip are your jam, there's no reason to think twice about making a meal out of them.

5 SLICES OF CUCUMBER

5 CARROT STICKS

5 PITA CHIPS

3 TABLESPOONS TZATZIKI

3 TABLESPOONS HUMMUS

3 TABLESPOONS ARTICHOKE DIP

Arrange the cucumber, carrots, and chips on a plate, making sure to leave some space between them.

Fill the spaces with the tzatziki, hummus, and artichoke dip and enjoy.

NO NAANSENSE

Pillowy naan, a refreshing and nutritious salad, and a warming bowl of chana masala—sometimes all you need is something simple that makes you feel energized and rejuvenated.

1 (10 OZ.) BAG OF CHANA MASALA

1 CUP SPRING MIX

1 TABLESPOON DRIED CRANBERRIES

1 TABLESPOON CHOPPED DRIED APRICOTS

PREFERRED DRESSING, AS DESIRED

1 PIECE OF NAAN

Cook the chana masala according to the directions on the package.

Place the spring mix, cranberries, and apricots in a bowl, drizzle the dressing over the top, and toss to combine.

Serve the chana masala alongside the salad and naan and enjoy.

TOTAL TIME: 15 MINUTES

EVEN I'M IMPRESSED

The girl dinner phenomenon is all about making the easy road artful, but that doesn't mean that results can't reach high levels. Take this meal, which is easy to put together, and as appealing to the eye as it is to the tastebuds.

¼ LB. COOKED AND PULLED CHICKEN

1 TABLESPOON FAJITA SEASONING

½ CUP REFRIED BLACK BEANS

3 TOSTADAS

1 TEASPOON PEELED AND CHOPPED WATERMELON RADISH

HOT SAUCE, TO TASTE

1 TABLESPOON CRUMBLED COTIJA CHEESE

FRESH CILANTRO, CHOPPED, FOR GARNISH

Place the chicken in a pot, sprinkle the fajita seasoning over it, and add ¼ cup water. Bring to a gentle simmer and cook until the chicken is warmed through.

While the chicken is simmering, warm the refried beans according to the directions on the package.

Arrange the tostadas on a plate and top them with the refried beans, chicken, radish, hot sauce, and cotija cheese. Garnish with cilantro and enjoy.

MEZZE MASTERPIECE

The mezze platter might be at the core of Mediterranean cuisine, but it has fans all over the world. Join the legions who love its combination of tastes and textures with this spread.

1 CUP TABBOULEH

1 MINIATURE CUCUMBER, SLICED

1 TO 3 BABY BELL PEPPERS, STEMMED, SEEDED, AND CHOPPED

6 TO 8 PITA CHIPS

5 TO 8 CHERRY TOMATOES, SLICED

½ OZ. FETA CHEESE

¼ CUP HUMMUS

4 TO 6 MARINATED OLIVES

PAPRIKA, TO TASTE

SALT, TO TASTE

FRESH HERBS, CHOPPED, FOR GARNISH

Arrange the tabbouleh, cucumber, peppers, pita chips, tomatoes, feta, hummus, and olives on a plate. Sprinkle the paprika over the hummus and season everything with salt.

Garnish with fresh herbs and enjoy.

TOTAL RESET

Sometimes, you need to get down to brass tacks, and get your house in order. This collection does just that, offering protein, vitamins, fiber, and healthy fats for a complete and well-balanced meal. There's even a small reward for your commitment, in the form of an oatmeal cookie.

1 APPLE, CORED AND SLICED

¼ CUP COTTAGE CHEESE

¼ CUP NUTS

1 TEASPOON SEA SALT

HONEY, FOR DRIZZLING (OPTIONAL)

2 DATES

1 OATMEAL COOKIE

Place the apple, cottage cheese, and nuts in separate bowls. Sprinkle the salt over the cottage cheese and drizzle honey over the apple (if desired).

Arrange the bowls, dates, and oatmeal cookie on a board and enjoy.

POP OFF QUEEN

Girl dinner is great at helping you carve out space for a solid meal, but there are moments when the world conspires to make even that impossible. In these instances, turn to this effortless, portable, and revitalizing smoothie.

1 ORANGE POPSICLE, STICK REMOVED

¼ CUP FROZEN MANGO CHUNKS

¼ CUP FROZEN PINEAPPLE CHUNKS

½ CUP COCONUT WATER

1 TABLESPOON CHIA SEEDS

¼ CUP ICE

1 TABLESPOON HONEY

Place all of the ingredients in a blender and puree until smooth.

Pour the smoothie into a glass and enjoy.

OOH LA LA

Breakfast for dinner is always a comfort, but it can be elegant and wholesome as well, as shown in this Parisian-inspired spread.

1 FROZEN SINGLE-SERVING QUICHE

ARUGULA, AS DESIRED

1½ TEASPOONS EXTRA-VIRGIN OLIVE OIL

SALT AND PEPPER, TO TASTE

¼ CUP FRUIT

1 CUP WHOLE MILK, FRENCH-STYLE YOGURT

Cook the quiche according to the directions on the package.

Place the arugula in a bowl, add the olive oil, and season with salt and pepper. Toss to combine, serve the quiche alongside the salad, fruit, and yogurt, and enjoy.

LOVE THIS FOR ME

As the longevity enjoyed by the people who live around the Mediterranean has shown, the easiest move to make in the quest for better health is often just to incorporate more seafood into your diet.

1 SALMON FILLET (ABOUT 6 OZ.)

SALT, TO TASTE

½ LB. FROZEN RICE AND VEGETABLE BLEND

1 TABLESPOON CANOLA OIL

1½ TEASPOONS BLACKENING SPICE

About 20 minutes before you are going to cook the salmon, season it generously with salt. Let the salmon sit at room temperature.

Place the rice and vegetables in a pan, add ¼ cup water, and cook it over medium heat, scraping up any browned bits from the bottom of the pan. Cook until the rice and vegetables are warmed through, about 8 minutes.

Place the canola oil in a large cast-iron skillet and warm it over high heat. Pat the salmon dry and then coat it with the blackening spice.

Place the salmon in the pan and gently press down to ensure that it is lying flat in the pan.

Reduce the heat to medium-low and cook the salmon until the bottom is seared, about 5 minutes.

Turn the salmon over, turn off the heat, and let the salmon sit in the pan until it is cooked through, about 2 minutes.

Transfer the salmon to a cutting board and let it rest.

Place the rice and vegetables on a plate, top it with the salmon, and enjoy.

POST-WORKOUT PERFECTION

When you go hard in a workout, there's a real need to recharge afterward. This revitalizing blend makes that easy, wrapping energy-boosting and protein-packed ingredients in a delicious package.

½ FROZEN BANANA

1 SCOOP OF NO-SUGAR-ADDED VANILLA PROTEIN POWDER

½ CUP MILK

½ CUP ICED COFFEE

½ CUP ICE

1 TABLESPOON COCOA POWDER

1 PITTED DATE

1 TEASPOON PURE VANILLA EXTRACT

1 TEASPOON CINNAMON

Place all of the ingredients in a blender and puree until smooth.

Pour the smoothie into a glass and enjoy.

NOT JUST A SALAD

So often, a salad seems like something we default to—healthy, sure, but difficult to get hyped about. This salad preserves the dish's best aspects—healthy and refreshing—and adds a reason to get excited: the rich flavor of carne asada.

1 SERVING OF CARNE ASADA-MARINATED BEEF

½ CUP ARUGULA

1 TABLESPOON EXTRA-VIRGIN OLIVE OIL

1 TABLESPOON FRESH LIME JUICE

SALT AND PEPPER, TO TASTE

3 TABLESPOONS GUACAMOLE

¼ CUP PICO DE GALLO

5 CHERRY TOMATOES

Warm a grill pan over high heat. Add the beef and cook until it is seared on both sides and cooked to the desired level of doneness, turning it over just once.

Remove the beef from the pan and let it rest for 5 minutes.

Place the arugula in a bowl, add the olive oil and lime juice, and season with salt and pepper. Toss to combine and transfer the salad to a plate.

Top the salad with the guacamole, pico de gallo, and cherry tomatoes.

Slice the beef, arrange it on top of the salad, and enjoy.

BIG MOOD

Bringing home some premade skewers from the store is a great option when you don't have any time—or energy—to prep, but you want something that is comforting, delicious, and healthy.

1 SERVING OF CHICKEN & VEGETABLE KEBABS

¼ CUP THAI CHILE GLAZE

Preheat the oven to 375°F and coat a baking sheet with nonstick cooking spray. Arrange the kebabs on the baking sheet and place it in the oven. Roast until the chicken is cooked through (the internal temperature is 165°F), 15 to 20 minutes.

Remove the kebabs from the oven, serve with the Thai chile glaze, and enjoy.

SUNDAY KIND OF LOVE

After a busy weekend, all one wants is to spend Sunday sitting at home, eating good food, and recharging for the week ahead. This spread, which would also be great as a late lunch, helps you accomplish both goals with ease.

4 TO 6 GREEK MEATBALLS

3 TO 4 PIECES OF NAAN

1 MINIATURE CUCUMBER, SLICED

¼ SMALL ONION, SLICED

¼ CUP TZATZIKI

FRESH DILL, CHOPPED, FOR GARNISH

Preheat the oven to 350°F and coat a baking sheet with nonstick cooking spray. Place the meatballs on the baking sheet and place them in the oven. Bake until the meatballs are browned and cooked through, 12 to 15 minutes, turning them as necessary.

Remove the meatballs from the oven. Arrange the meatballs, naan, cucumber, onion, and tzatziki on a plate, garnish with dill, and enjoy.

PEAS AND THANK YOU

When you're looking to focus on wellness, a plant-based dinner is always a good option. Sure, but what about the protein? you might ask. This vegan option removes that rightful concern, turning to protein-packed lentils and chickpeas to round things out.

½ CUP MICROWAVABLE LENTILS

SALT, TO TASTE

¼ CUP CANNED CHICKPEAS

¼ CUP DICED ROASTED BEETS

6 TO 8 CARROT CHIPS

10 TO 12 SUGAR SNAP PEAS

SPROUTS, GREENS, OR SPRING MIX, AS DESIRED

Cook the lentils according to the directions on the package. When they have finished cooking, season them with salt.

Arrange all of the items on a board or a plate—have fun and don't be afraid to get creative. One idea if you are stuck: overlap the carrot chips and peas, place the chickpeas in a ramekin, and top the lentils with the beets.

MAIN CHARACTER ENERGY

This inventive fusion of Mediterranean and Latin American cuisines brings to mind a ceviche, only a plant-based one. It's a great dish to turn to if you need a salad, but are also in the mood for something with a bit more panache.

2 TABLESPOONS DIJON MUSTARD

½ TEASPOON GARLIC CONFIT

6 OLIVES, HALVED

¼ CUP MARINATED ARTICHOKE HEARTS

¼ CUP SLICED HEARTS OF PALM

2 TABLESPOONS DICED SUN-DRIED TOMATOES IN OLIVE OIL

1 TEASPOON CAPERS

1 TEASPOON FINELY CHOPPED FRESH PARSLEY

2 TABLESPOONS GARLIC CONFIT OIL

SALT AND PEPPER, TO TASTE

Place the mustard and garlic confit in a mixing bowl and mash to combine.

Add the remaining ingredients and toss to combine.

Place the "ceviche" in a glass bowl and enjoy.

THE BRUNCH BUNCH

Brimming with omega-3s, antioxidants, and protein, this brunch-inspired collection of offerings will come through anytime, anywhere.

2 EGGS

½ PACKAGE OF SMOKED SALMON

FLESH OF ½ AVOCADO, SLICED

5 CUCUMBER SLICES

EVERYTHING SEASONING, TO TASTE

¼ CUP COTTAGE CHEESE

HANDFUL OF BLUEBERRIES

SALT, TO TASTE

TOAST, FOR SERVING (OPTIONAL)

Prepare an ice bath. Bring a medium saucepan of water to a boil. Add the eggs and, when the water returns to a boil, set a timer for 9 minutes.

Cook the eggs until the timer goes off. Remove the eggs from the boiling water and transfer them to the ice bath. Let the eggs cool completely.

Gently crack the eggs' shells and peel the eggs. Halve the eggs lengthwise and arrange them on a board with the smoked salmon, avocado, and cucumber.

Sprinkle everything seasoning over the eggs.

Place the cottage cheese in a small bowl, top it with the blueberries, and season it with salt.

Serve with the toast (if desired) and enjoy.

I BEAN EVERYWHERE

Buttery, sweet, and spicy, this well-balanced bean salad is a great preparation to turn to when you want a lot of flavor without having to do a lot of work.

1 TABLESPOON EXTRA-VIRGIN OLIVE OIL

1 BAG OF FROZEN CORN

SALT AND PEPPER, TO TASTE

1 (14 OZ.) CAN OF BLACK BEANS, DRAINED

FLESH OF ½ AVOCADO, DICED

3 TABLESPOONS DICED TOMATOES

JUICE OF ½ LIME

FRESH CILANTRO, FOR GARNISH

JALAPEÑO CHILE PEPPER, SLICED, FOR GARNISH

Place the olive oil in a large skillet and warm it over medium heat. Add the corn and cook, stirring occasionally, until it is warmed through. Season the corn with salt and pepper and transfer it to a serving bowl.

Add the black beans, avocado, tomatoes, and lime juice to the bowl and season the mixture with salt and pepper. Toss to combine.

Garnish the salad with cilantro and jalapeño and enjoy.

THERE ARE FEW BETTER WAYS TO MARK A SPECIAL OCCASION THAN THROUGH FOOD THAT EMBODIES THE SPIRIT OF THE MOMENT. THIS CHAPTER HELPS YOU CELEBRATE EVERY EVENT, WHETHER IT'S A HOLIDAY OR JUST AN EVERYDAY OCCURRENCE THAT DESERVES TO FEEL A LITTLE ELEVATED. WE ENCOURAGE YOU TO DELIGHT NOT ONLY IN THE DAYS THAT EVERYONE ACKNOWLEDGES, BUT IN THE MUNDANE MOMENTS THAT ARE ALL TOO EASY TO WRITE OFF AS ORDINARY. ROMANTICIZE YOUR ROUTINE, AND YOU WILL BE SURPRISED TO FIND WHAT A DIFFERENCE IT MAKES IN YOUR MINDSET.

APRÈS APPLE PICKING

When fall's crisp air and golden light descend, there's no better place to spend a day than an apple orchard. Once you're back home, maintain the day's comforting, wholesome warmth with this spread of apple-infused preparations.

APPLE CIDER DOUGHNUTS, AS DESIRED

APPLE-SMOKED BACON, COOKED, AS DESIRED

1 APPLE, CORED

APPLE BUTTER, AS DESIRED

Arrange the doughnuts on one side of the plate and the bacon on the opposite side.

Slice or dice the apple and arrange it around the plate.

Add some apple butter to the plate and enjoy.

RED, WHITE, AND BLUE-TIFUL

Putting a patriotic spin on a delightful collection of treats is a wonderful way to celebrate the 4th of July, and match the fireworks displays with something equally spectacular.

16 SLICES OF SALAMI

¼ CUP BLUEBERRIES

2 TABLESPOONS STRAWBERRY JAM

¼ CUP POPCORN

¼ CUP NUTS

1 COOKIE

2 ROUNDS OF BABYBEL CHEESE

4 PINEAPPLE CHUNKS

HANDFUL OF PRETZELS

Fold a slice of salami in half, and then fold it again, creating a fan shape. Repeat with the remaining salami slices.

Arrange the salami in the middle of a board or plate so that they spell out "USA."

Place the blueberries and jam in separate ramekins and set them on the board or plate. Arrange the remaining ingredients and enjoy.

GOURD SEASON

When fall hits, it's time to get as much pumpkin and apple as you can. This quick dinner supplies your daily fix of both, and the salad provides the necessary counter to the richness of the brown butter-coated ravioli.

2 TABLESPOONS UNSALTED BUTTER

4 PUMPKIN RAVIOLI

1 CUP SPRING MIX

1½ TEASPOONS EXTRA-VIRGIN OLIVE OIL

SALT, TO TASTE

8 SLICES OF APPLE

WALNUTS, FOR GARNISH

HONEY, FOR DRIZZLING

Bring a large saucepan of water to a boil.

While the water is coming to a boil, place the butter in a skillet and melt it over medium-low heat. Cook until it starts to brown and gives off a nutty aroma, 6 to 8 minutes. Remove the pan from heat and set the brown butter aside.

Add the ravioli to the boiling water and cook until they are al dente, 6 to 8 minutes. Drain the ravioli, add them to the brown butter, and toss to coat.

Place the spring mix in a bowl, add the olive oil, and season with salt. Toss to coat and arrange the salad on a plate with the ravioli and apple slices. Top with walnuts, drizzle honey over the apple slices, and enjoy.

IT'S ON AND POPPIN'

If you're a sports fanatic and are looking for something that elevates the experience of watching at home, whip up these treats before tuning in.

1 SERVING OF FROZEN BUFFALO-STYLE CHICKEN POPPERS

2 TABLESPOONS CRUMBLED BLUE CHEESE

HOT SAUCE, AS DESIRED

10 TO 12 CARROT STICKS

8 TO 10 CELERY STICKS

Cook the poppers according to the directions on the package.

Place the blue cheese in a ramekin and the hot sauce in another one.

Remove the poppers from the oven and let them cool for about 5 minutes.

Arrange them on a plate with the ramekins, carrots, and celery and enjoy.

GET READY WITH ME

A sophisticated and speedy dinner that will allow you to focus on getting ready for a big night on the town, and help you make the most of it once you're out.

5 CRACKERS

¼ CUP CREAM CHEESE

10 SLICES OF CUCUMBER

5 PIECES OF SMOKED SALMON

8 TO 10 SLICES OF RED ONION

EVERYTHING SEASONING, TO TASTE

Arrange the crackers on a board and spread some cream cheese on each cracker.

Top each cracker with 2 slices of cucumber, 1 piece of smoked salmon, and 2 slices of red onion. Sprinkle everything seasoning over the top and enjoy.

THE HOLIDAY

Toss on your favorite Christmas movie and kick back with this hearty and satisfying treat that effortlessly captures the spirit of the holidays.

1 TABLESPOON CHOPPED TOASTED PECANS

1 TEASPOON DRIED CRANBERRIES

1 TEASPOON DICED APPLE

¼ TEASPOON FINELY CHOPPED FRESH SAGE

1 TEASPOON HONEY

¼ TEASPOON CINNAMON

1 TABLESPOON APPLE BUTTER OR APPLESAUCE

ZEST AND JUICE OF 1 LEMON

2 PINCHES OF KOSHER SALT

1 TEASPOON UNSALTED BUTTER

1 THICK SLICE OF SOURDOUGH BREAD

3 TO 4 SLICES WHITE STILTON CRANBERRY CHEESE (ABOUT 2 OZ.)

Place all of the ingredients, except for the butter, bread, and Stilton, in a bowl and stir until well combined. Set the mixture aside.

Place the butter in a skillet and melt it over medium heat. Add the bread and toast until it is golden brown on both sides, turning it as necessary.

Place the toast on a plate and top it with the Stilton. Top the Stilton with the topping mixture and enjoy.

SUMMERTIME SADNESS

The advent of zucchini noodles have been a godsend for the carb-conscious pasta lover, allowing them to indulge without worry. Here they form the base of this wonderful summer dish, which was made for those evenings when you feel autumn creeping in.

1 TABLESPOON EXTRA-VIRGIN OLIVE OIL

1 LINK OF CHICKEN SAUSAGE, SLICED

1 SERVING OF ZUCCHINI NOODLES

¼ CUP CHERRY TOMATOES

¼ CUP CANNED CHICKPEAS, DRAINED

½ CUP TOMATO SAUCE

1 TEASPOON ITALIAN SEASONING

1 TEASPOON KOSHER SALT

PARMESAN CHEESE, SHAVED, FOR GARNISH

FRESH BASIL, FOR GARNISH

Place the olive oil in a pan and warm it over medium-high heat. Add the sausage and cook until it is browned all over and cooked through, stirring occasionally, 6 to 8 minutes. Remove the sausage from the pan and set it aside.

Add the zucchini noodles to the pan and cook, stirring occasionally, until they are tender, about 5 minutes.

Add the tomatoes and chickpeas to the pan and cook, stirring occasionally, until they start to brown, about 5 minutes.

Add the sauce, Italian seasoning, and salt, return the chicken sausage to the pan, and cook until everything is warmed through. Taste and adjust the seasoning as necessary.

Transfer the dish to a plate, top it with Parmesan and basil, and enjoy.

MOVIE NIGHT

When all you want is to curl up on the couch and watch a movie, turn to this preparation, which features a tried-and-true girl dinner stratagem: use some stemware to add elegance to the proceedings.

1 CUP POPCORN

¼ CUP TRAIL MIX

3 TO 5 CHEDDAR SLICES

5 TO 8 SALAMI SLICES

¼ CUP PRETZELS

Place the popcorn in a coupe or a wineglass and arrange it on a plate or a board.

Arrange the remaining ingredients around the popcorn and enjoy.

GET A LITTLE PIZZA MIND

Are your tastebuds clamoring for pizza? This spread is sure to soothe that craving, and do so in a much lighter and more balanced manner.

1 BOX OF FROZEN PIZZA BITES

10 TO 12 SLICES OF PEPPERONI

1 BURRATA

2 TABLESPOONS SLICED BANANA PEPPERS

3 TO 5 MARINATED ARTICHOKE HEARTS, HALVED

PARMESAN CHEESE, GRATED, FOR GARNISH

Cook the pizza bites according to the directions on the package.

Arrange the pizza bites and the remaining ingredients on a board and enjoy.

CATCH ME POOLSIDE

When you get a chance to have a day where nothing more is on the docket than lounging by the pool, this delicious spread comes in handy, allowing you to linger as long as you want, since a delicious dinner is just minutes away.

1 PACKAGE OF CARNE ASADA-MARINATED BEEF

½ CUP MICROWAVABLE RICE

¼ CUP GUACAMOLE

¼ CUP PICO DE GALLO

2 TO 3 TORTILLAS

LIME WEDGES

Warm a grill pan over high heat. Add the beef and cook until it is seared on both sides and cooked to the desired level of doneness, turning it over just once.

Remove the beef from the pan and let it rest for 5 minutes.

While the beef is resting, cook the rice according to the directions on the package.

Slice the beef, serve it alongside the rice, guacamole, pico de gallo, and tortillas, and enjoy.

STILL THANKS TO GIVE

The best part of Thanksgiving is all of those leftovers, which preserve the warm feelings of the holiday and provide ample fuel for you to tackle the start of shopping season.

THANKSGIVING LEFTOVERS, AS DESIRED

Warm over your leftovers, arrange them on a board in a creative and festive manner, and enjoy.

PUMPKIN SPICE SEASON

Are you one of those people who can't get enough pumpkin spice once the weather turns cold? Of course you are. Lean into your one true love with this girl dinner.

1 CUP PEELED, SEEDED, AND DICED BUTTERNUT SQUASH

½ TEASPOON KOSHER SALT

¼ TEASPOON CINNAMON

1 TABLESPOON EXTRA-VIRGIN OLIVE OIL

1 TEASPOON HONEY

¼ TEASPOON BLACK PEPPER

1 (10.5 OZ.) CAN OF PUMPKIN SOUP

PREFERRED DRESSING, AS DESIRED

1 TABLESPOON PEPITAS

2 CUPS SPRING MIX

PUMPKIN SPICE LATTE, FOR SERVING

Preheat the oven to 375°F. Place the squash in a bowl, add the salt, cinnamon, olive oil, honey, and pepper, and toss to combine. Transfer the squash to a baking sheet and place it in the oven. Roast until the squash is tender and browned, about 40 minutes.

While the squash is in the oven, warm the soup according to the directions on the package.

Remove the squash from the oven, transfer it to a bowl, and add the dressing and pepitas. Toss to combine, add the spring mix, and gently toss to combine.

Serve the salad alongside the soup and enjoy with a pumpkin spice latte.

SPA NIGHT

Need to treat yourself? Transform the evening into something out of a spa retreat with these light, revitalizing, and creative rolls.

1 (5 OZ.) CAN OF TUNA, DRAINED

¼ CUP HUMMUS

½ TEASPOON DIJON MUSTARD

JUICE OF ½ LEMON

SALT AND PEPPER, TO TASTE

1 SMALL ENGLISH CUCUMBER

FRESH DILL, CHOPPED, FOR GARNISH

Place the tuna in a bowl and flake it with a fork. Add the hummus and mustard and work the mixture until it is combined. Add the lemon juice, season the tuna with salt and pepper, and stir to incorporate. Taste and adjust the seasoning as necessary.

Trim the ends from the cucumber and then use a mandoline or a vegetable peeler to slice it into long, thin strips. Slice until you reach the center, turn the cucumber over, and repeat on the other side. Discard the initial slices made on both sides.

Spread the tuna over the strips of cucumber and roll them up.

Arrange the rolls on a plate, placing them seam side down, garnish with dill, and enjoy.

SPRING IN YOUR STEP

Celebrate the annual miracle of the world returning to life with this vegetable-packed group of bites.

1 MINIATURE CUCUMBER

2 TO 4 SMALL PIECES OF KALE

2 TO 4 SMALL SPINACH LEAVES

3 TO 5 CHERRY TOMATOES

1 RADISH, SLICED

2 BABY BELL PEPPERS, STEMMED, SEEDED, AND QUARTERED

2 TABLESPOONS CANNED CHICKPEAS

BALSAMIC VINEGAR, FOR DRIZZLING

EXTRA-VIRGIN OLIVE OIL, FOR DRIZZLING

SALT, TO TASTE

Trim the ends from the cucumber and then use a mandoline or a vegetable peeler to slice it into 6 long, thin strips. Discard the initial slice made and set the other slices aside.

Arrange the kale and spinach in a line in the middle of a round plate.

Arrange the tomatoes, radish, peppers, cucumber, and chickpeas on top of the kale and spinach, getting creative with how you display and overlap the ingredients.

Drizzle balsamic and olive oil over the dish, season it with salt, and enjoy.

OH DIP

Savor the sensations of summer with this intriguing presentation of dips.

½ CUP GUACAMOLE

¼ CUP SALSA ROJA

½ CUP PICO DE GALLO

TORTILLA CHIPS, FOR SERVING

Grab a tumbler or a mason jar and layer the ingredients in it. We recommend starting with the guacamole on the bottom, then adding the salsa roja, and finishing with the pico de gallo.

Serve with tortilla chips and enjoy.

UNDER THE WEATHER

When you're not feeling great, make this meal and get to bed early to put yourself on the road to a quick recovery.

1 (10.5 OZ.) CAN OF SOUP

5 TO 7 TORTELLINI

1 CUP KALE LEAVES, RINSED WELL

2 TABLESPOONS GRATED PARMESAN CHEESE

3 TABLESPOONS CAESAR DRESSING

Place the soup in a small saucepan and bring it to a simmer. Add the tortellini and simmer until they are cooked through, 7 to 9 minutes.

While the tortellini are cooking, place the kale, Parmesan, and Caesar dressing in a bowl and toss to combine.

Serve the salad alongside the soup and tortellini and enjoy.

YOU SAY TOMATO

When tomato season arrives, the challenge becomes finding as many ways as possible to celebrate it. While there are many recipes that can do this, few are better than this collection, and none that can be prepared quicker.

10 TO 12 CHERRY TOMATOES

1 MINIATURE CUCUMBER, SLICED

¼ CUP MINIATURE MOZZARELLA BALLS

5 FRESH BASIL LEAVES

BALSAMIC VINEGAR, FOR DRIZZLING

EXTRA-VIRGIN OLIVE OIL, FOR DRIZZLING

SALT, TO TASTE

Halve 5 of the tomatoes and leave the rest whole. Arrange the tomatoes, cucumber, mozzarella balls, and basil on a plate, getting creative with the arrangement.

Drizzle balsamic and olive oil over the top, sprinkle with salt, and enjoy.

GALENTINE'S EXTRAVANGZA

If you've got no plans on Valentine's Day, show yourself some self-love with this indulgent spread. And if you are celebrating the holiday with someone, just double the amounts recommended below, and make it a night to remember.

5 SLICES OF BAGUETTE

EXTRA-VIRGIN OLIVE OIL, TO TASTE

5 SLICES OF PROSCIUTTO

¼ CUP BOURSIN CHEESE

1 TO 2 TABLESPOONS STRAWBERRY PRESERVES

HONEY, FOR DRIZZLING

TOASTED NUTS, FOR GARNISH

Preheat the oven to 400°F and line a baking sheet with parchment paper. Place the slices of baguette on the baking sheet and brush both sides with olive oil. Place the baguette in the oven and toast until it is golden brown on each side, 10 to 12 minutes, turning the slices over halfway through.

While you are toasting the baguette, take 1 slice of prosciutto and fold it in half lengthwise. Twist the prosciutto and then gently separate the top, so that it resembles a rose. Repeat with the rest of the prosciutto.

Remove the crostini from the oven and spread the Boursin over 3 of them. Spread the strawberry preserves over the remaining slices. Top each crostini with a prosciutto rose and arrange them on a board.

Drizzle honey over the crostini and serve with nuts.

LIVING FOR LEFTOVERS

After the onslaught of Thanksgiving, one can't help but seek out lighter meals. This accomplishes that task, capturing the beloved flavors of the season without immediately sending you to the couch for a nap.

1 TABLESPOON UNSALTED BUTTER

1 THICK SLICE OF SOURDOUGH BREAD

1 TABLESPOON CRANBERRY RELISH

3 TO 4 SLICES OF LEFTOVER TURKEY

3 SLICES OF BRIE CHEESE (ABOUT 2 OZ.)

Preheat the oven to 400°F and coat a baking sheet with the butter.

Place the bread on the baking sheet and spread the cranberry relish over the bread. Place the sliced turkey on the bread and top it with the Brie.

Place the sandwich in the oven and bake until the bread is toasted, the turkey is warmed through, and the Brie has softened.

Remove the sandwich from the oven and enjoy.

TOTAL TIME: 10 TO 15 MINUTES

TAILGATE GATEKEEP GIRLBOSS

Tailgating is the best part of going to a football game, but it's surprisingly easy to hit that same height at home.

1 BRATWURST OR HOT DOG

½ CUP SPINACH LEAVES

3 TO 5 CARROT CHIPS

½ MINIATURE CUCUMBER, SLICED

½ RADISH, SLICED

SALT, TO TASTE

1 HOT DOG BUN

1 TABLESPOON BALSAMIC VINAIGRETTE

POTATO CHIPS, FOR SERVING

Cook the bratwurst or hot dog on the stove or in the oven until it is browned all over and cooked through (the internal temperature is 165°F).

While the bratwurst or hot dog is cooking, place the spinach, carrots, cucumber, and radish in a bowl. Season with salt and toss to combine.

Place the bratwurst or hot dog in the bun. Drizzle the vinaigrette over the salad. Arrange the bratwurst or hot dog, the salad, and potato chips on a plate and enjoy.

GOOD COMPANY

WHILE GIRL DINNER IS A GREAT WAY TO TREAT YOURSELF AND ENJOY SOME ALONE TIME, SOMETIMES THE BEST GIRL DINNERS ARE THE ONES YOU SHARE WITH OTHERS. THERE'S NOTHING QUITE LIKE ENJOYING A MEAL WITH THE PEOPLE YOU LOVE MOST. WHETHER IT BE FOR A FAMILY FUNCTION, A ROMANTIC EVENING, OR A GETAWAY WITH THE GIRLS, SOMETIMES PREPARING A SIMPLE MEAL IS THE PERFECT WAY TO SHOW YOU CARE. AND WITH LITTLE TO NO COOKING INVOLVED, THESE DISHES LEAVE YOU THAT MUCH MORE TIME TO SPEND WITH YOUR LOVED ONES.

ALL I CARE ABOUT IS PASTA AND LIKE THREE PEOPLE

Composed of items that you likely already have on hand, this time-less meal is great for sharing with a few friends. Depending on everyone's hunger level, expect the amounts given below to feed four to six people.

1 BAG OF FROZEN ITALIAN MEATBALLS

SALT AND PEPPER, TO TASTE

1 LB. SPAGHETTI

4 CUPS MARINARA SAUCE

ITALIAN SEASONING, TO TASTE

¼ CUP SHAVED PARMESAN CHEESE

Preheat the oven to 350°F and position a rack in the middle. Place the meatballs on a baking sheet and bake until they are cooked through, 15 to 20 minutes, turning them over halfway through.

While the meatballs are in the oven, bring a large saucepan of water to a boil. Add salt and the spaghetti and cook until the spaghetti is al dente, 8 to 12 minutes. Drain the spaghetti and set it aside.

Place the sauce in the pan and bring it to a simmer. Taste, season with salt, pepper, and Italian seasoning, and add the spaghetti. Toss to combine.

Remove the meatballs from the oven and add them to the spaghetti. Toss to incorporate and serve, topping each portion with some of the Parmesan.

GIRLS' NIGHT IN

If you and a few friends (the preparation will work for a group of two to four people) are hunkering down and taking shelter from the brutal winter weather, spiking some mac and cheese with chili is a great way to keep things cozy.

1 (6 OZ.) BOX OF MAC AND CHEESE

1 (14 OZ.) CAN OF CHILI

CHEDDAR OR PREFERRED CHEESE, SHREDDED, FOR TOPPING

Cook the mac and cheese according to the directions on the package.

Place the chili in a saucepan and warm it over medium heat.

Add the chili to the mac and cheese and stir to combine.

Top the mac and cheese with shredded cheese and enjoy.

FOR THE BOOK CLUB

When it's your turn to host the book club, turn to this baked Brie recipe, which is a harmonious blend of sweet and savory. This recipe should comfortably feed a group of four, so adjust the amounts based on the size of your group.

⅓ CUP CHOPPED PECANS

¼ CUP DRIED CRANBERRIES

¼ CUP DICED APPLES

1 TABLESPOON FINELY CHOPPED FRESH SAGE

½ TEASPOON CINNAMON

¼ CUP HONEY

1 TABLESPOON APPLE BUTTER

2 PINCHES OF KOSHER SALT

ZEST AND JUICE OF 1 LEMON

1 WHEEL OF BRIE CHEESE

BREAD OR CRACKERS, FOR SERVING

Preheat the oven to 350°F and line a baking sheet with parchment paper.

Place the pecans, cranberries, apples, sage, and cinnamon in a bowl and toss to combine. Add the honey, apple butter, salt, and lemon zest and juice and stir to combine.

Place the Brie on the baking sheet and spread the topping over it. Place the Brie in the oven and bake until it has softened slightly, about 12 minutes.

Remove the Brie from the oven and let it rest for 3 minutes. Serve with bread or crackers and enjoy.

DATE NIGHT

This dinner lets you enjoy a special evening where you get the chance to focus on one another. Avoid having to spend time apart as you toil away in the kitchen with this simple but romantic dinner.

3 TO 4 TABLESPOONS UNSALTED BUTTER

1 TABLESPOON EXTRA-VIRGIN OLIVE OIL

½ LB. FROZEN CAULIFLOWER GNOCCHI, THAWED

SALT, TO TASTE

ITALIAN SEASONING, TO TASTE

1 BURRATA

Place the butter in a skillet and melt it over medium-low heat. Cook it until it starts to brown and gives off a nutty aroma, 6 to 8 minutes. Remove the pan from heat and set the brown butter aside.

Place the olive oil in a large skillet and warm it over medium-high heat. Working in batches to avoid crowding the pan, add the gnocchi and cook until the bottoms are golden brown, about 3 minutes. Turn the gnocchi over and cook until they are browned on both sides.

Remove the gnocchi from the pan and season them with salt and Italian seasoning. Add them to the brown butter and toss to coat.

Place the burrata in the center of a serving plate and pull it open. Arrange the gnocchi around the burrata and enjoy.

FOR MY BESTIES

Baked feta has gained considerable momentum on social media of late, and using it in this visually stunning and flavorful dish is sure to set you and your friends—two to four, ideally—similarly abuzz.

1 CUP CHERRY TOMATOES

4 BABY BELL PEPPERS, STEMMED, SEEDED, AND QUARTERED

3 GARLIC CLOVES, SMASHED

1 TABLESPOON EXTRA-VIRGIN OLIVE OIL

¼ TEASPOON KOSHER SALT

BLACK PEPPER, TO TASTE

4 OZ. FETA CHEESE

9 OZ. HEARTS OF PALM PASTA

1 TEASPOON DRIED HERBS

2 PINCHES OF RED PEPPER FLAKES

Preheat the oven to 400°F. Place the tomatoes, bell peppers, and garlic in a baking dish, drizzle the olive oil over the mixture, and season with the salt and pepper. Toss to coat and then arrange the feta in the center of the baking dish.

Place the dish in the oven and roast until the tomatoes have burst, about 40 minutes.

While the vegetables are roasting, cook the pasta according to the directions on the package.

Remove the dish from the oven and add the cooked pasta, herbs, and red pepper flakes to the vegetables and feta. Toss to combine and enjoy.

A BOND LIKE NO OTHER

If you and a friend are two people who cannot get enough carbs, then this savory, tangy, and nutty main was made for you both.

1 LB. BAG OF FROZEN QUINOA & COUSCOUS BLEND

1 TABLESPOON MASHED GARLIC

¼ CUP MARINATED ARTICHOKE HEARTS

ZEST OF 1 LEMON

1½ TEASPOONS EXTRA-VIRGIN OLIVE OIL

1 TABLESPOON CRUMBLED FETA CHEESE

SALT AND PEPPER, TO TASTE

Cook the quinoa and couscous according to the directions on the package, stirring in the garlic.

Transfer the mixture to a bowl and add the remaining ingredients. Toss to combine and enjoy.

HOT TAKE

Two of the best developments of the contemporary culinary revolution—elevating ramen from its place as the dorm room default, and the sublime comfort of birria—are brought together in this bold and irresistible dish, which makes an ideal dinner for two people.

2 EGGS

1 CUP STORE-BOUGHT BEEF BIRRIA

2 (3 OZ.) PACKAGES OF INSTANT RAMEN

2 TEASPOONS CHILI-GARLIC SAUCE

FRESH CILANTRO, FOR GARNISH

LIME WEDGES, FOR SERVING

Prepare an ice bath. Bring a medium saucepan of water to a boil. Add the eggs and, when the water returns to a boil, set a timer for 9 minutes.

Cook the eggs until the timer goes off. Remove the eggs from the boiling water and transfer them to the ice bath. Let the eggs cool completely.

Gently crack the eggs' shells and peel the eggs. Halve the eggs lengthwise and set them aside.

Warm the birria in a saucepan and cook the ramen according to the directions on the package.

Divide the ramen and birria between two bowls and top each portion with an egg and some chili-garlic sauce. Garnish with cilantro, serve with lime wedges, and enjoy.

EVERYBODY'S DOING IT

Whipped feta is seemingly everywhere on social media lately, and this recipe allows you and three to five friends to discover what all of the fuss is about.

6 OZ. FETA CHEESE

⅓ CUP GREEK YOGURT

2 TABLESPOONS EXTRA-VIRGIN OLIVE OIL

1 TEASPOON OLIVE BRINE

ZEST OF 1 LEMON

JUICE OF ½ LEMON

SALT AND PEPPER, TO TASTE

1 TEASPOON RED PEPPER FLAKES

1 TABLESPOON CHOPPED PISTACHIOS

HONEY, FOR DRIZZLING

BREAD OR CRACKERS, FOR SERVING

Place the feta and Greek yogurt in a food processor and blitz until the mixture is smooth and airy, scraping down the work bowl as necessary.

Add the olive oil, olive brine, lemon zest, and lemon juice and blitz to incorporate. Season the whipped feta with salt and transfer it to a shallow bowl.

Top it with pepper, the red pepper flakes, pistachios, and honey, serve with bread or crackers, and enjoy.

SCREAM QUEEN

Indulge in your dark side when putting this spooky spread together. It's intended to serve two people, so make sure that whoever you share it with doesn't scare easily.

1 SMALL PLASTIC SKELETON, FOR DECORATION

3 TO 5 SLICES OF PROSCIUTTO

10 TO 12 SLICES OF SALAMI

6 SLICES OF CHEDDAR CHEESE

PREFERRED ACCOMPANIMENTS, AS DESIRED

Grab a medium-sized board and arrange the plastic skeleton in the middle so that it is sitting on the board.

Wrap the skeleton's arms and torso with the prosciutto. Cover the legs with the salami.

Arrange the cheddar cheese and any other accompaniments around the skeleton and enjoy.

TACO TWOS-DAY

Turn any evening into taco night with this speedy twist on tacos al pastor. It's intended to serve two, but no one would blame you if you decided to keep it all for yourself.

½ LB. LEFTOVER ROASTED PORK BELLY

8 CORN TORTILLAS

¼ CUP DICED PINEAPPLE

¼ CUP DICED PICKLED RED ONION

¼ CUP CRUMBLED QUESO FRESCO

¼ CUP SALSA ROJA

FRESH CILANTRO, CHOPPED, FOR GARNISH

Place the pork belly in a skillet and cook it over medium-high heat until it is crispy outside and warmed through, turning it as necessary.

Transfer the pork belly to a cutting board and dice it.

Place the tortillas in the pan and toast them on each side for 30 to 45 seconds.

Stack 2 tortillas on top of each other. Top each stack with some pork belly, pineapple, pickled onion, queso fresco, and salsa, garnish with cilantro. Repeat with the remaining ingredients and enjoy.

SOPHISTICATED SMORGASBORD

Getting together with some friends and trying out a few new bottles of wine is about as fun as the sophisticated adult world gets. And this collection of bites, which is good for a group of two or three people, is guaranteed to up everyone's enjoyment even further.

1 CHOCOLATE BAR, BROKEN INTO BITE-SIZE PIECES

ASSORTED CHEESES, SLICED OR CUBED

HANDFUL OF FIGS, HALVED OR QUARTERED

CRACKERS, AS DESIRED

¼ CUP FIG PRESERVES

Arrange all of the items on a board or plate—giving extra consideration to the look so that the meal screams elegance—and enjoy.

SPRING FLING

When spring has finally sprung, there is nothing better than a meal filled with nature's tastiest treats. This plate can comfortably serve two, for when you want to share the season's sunshine with a friend.

1 BURRATA

1 ORANGE, PEELED AND SEGMENTED

¼ CUP POMEGRANATE SEEDS

¼ APPLE, SLICED

¼ PEAR, SLICED

WALNUTS, FOR GARNISH

HONEY, FOR GARNISH

Place the burrata in the middle of a round plate. Arrange the fruit around the burrata, garnish with walnuts and honey, and enjoy.

NATURAL BEAUTY

This is intended for you and someone else who can't get enough of Mother Nature's bountiful gifts.

1 BAG OF FROZEN PEA, GREEN BEAN, AND BROCCOLI BLEND

4 SLICES OF PROSCIUTTO

¼ CUP CRUMBLED FETA CHEESE

SALT, TO TASTE

FRESH MINT, FOR GARNISH

Cook the vegetables according to the directions on the package.

While the vegetables are cooking, twist the prosciutto and set it aside.

Place the vegetables in a shallow bowl and top with the prosciutto and feta. Season with salt, garnish with mint, and enjoy.

METRIC CONVERSIONS

US MEASUREMENT	APPROXIMATE METRIC LIQUID MEASUREMENT	APPROXIMATE METRIC DRY MEASUREMENT
1 teaspoon	5 ml	5 g
1 tablespoon or ½ ounce	15 ml	14 g
1 ounce or ⅛ cup	30 ml	29 g
¼ cup or 2 ounces	60 ml	57 g
⅓ cup	80 ml	76 g
½ cup or 4 ounces	120 ml	113 g
⅔ cup	160 ml	151 g
¾ cup or 6 ounces	180 ml	170 g
1 cup or 8 ounces or ½ pint	240 ml	227 g
1½ cups or 12 ounces	350 ml	340 g
2 cups or 1 pint or 16 ounces	475 ml	454 g
3 cups or 1½ pints	700 ml	680 g
4 cups or 2 pints or 1 quart	950 ml	908 g

INDEX

ABOUT THE AUTHORS

Alejandra and Jamison are a wife-and-husband duo with a love for bringing restaurant-caliber recipes into the home kitchen. Having first met while working at a farm-to-table restaurant, they have a deep passion for the culinary industry that translates to their everyday lives.

Alejandra is a food photographer and stylist, and Jamie is a trained chef and recipe developer with 15+ years of experience at restaurants such as The Inn at Little Washington and Market Table Bistro. Together, they have authored two cookbooks: *Butter Boards: 50+ Inventive Spreads for Entertaining* and *Charcuterie by Occasion: 50 Versatile Seasonal Spreads*. With these cookbooks, Alejandra and Jamie bring their culinary expertise to the table, providing readers with a diverse range of ideas and recipes to make their next gathering a success.

Their blog, Off the Line, is packed with recipes that are fresh, feature seasonal ingredients, and integrate classic cooking techniques. The blog is focused on being approachable for the home cook, like Alejandra, and remarkable for the chef inside all of us, like Jamie.

Based in Northern Virginia, they enjoy visiting the best wineries and breweries around, taking daily walks, and exploring locally sourced ingredients. They believe that each meal, no matter how simple or elaborate, deserves to be a special moment that inspires.

ABOUT CIDER MILL PRESS BOOK PUBLISHERS

Good ideas ripen with time. From seed to harvest, Cider Mill Press brings fine reading, information, and entertainment together between the covers of its creatively crafted books. Our Cider Mill bears fruit twice a year, publishing a new crop of titles each spring and fall.

"Where Good Books Are Ready for Press"
501 Nelson Place
Nashville, Tennessee 37214

cidermillpress.com